HOORAY FOR GARBAGE COLLECTORS!

by Tessa Kenan

BUMBA BOOKS™

LERNER PUBLICATIONS ◆ MINNEAPOLIS

Note to Educators:

Throughout this book, you'll find critical thinking questions. These can be used to engage young readers in thinking critically about the topic and in using the text and photos to do so.

Lerner Publications Company
A division of Lerner Publishing Group, Inc.
241 First Avenue North
Minneapolis, MN 55401 USA

For reading levels and more information, look up this title at www.lernerbooks.com.

Library of Congress Cataloging-in-Publication Data

Names: Kenan, Tessa, author.
Title: Hooray for garbage collectors! / by Tessa Kenan.
Description: Minneapolis : Lerner Publications, [2018] | Series: Bumba books? Hooray for community helpers | Audience: Age 4–7. | Audience: Grade Pre-school, excluding K. | Includes bibliographical references and index.
Identifiers: LCCN 2016044369 (print) | LCCN 2017006447 (ebook) | ISBN 9781512433524 (lb : alk. paper) | ISBN 9781512455526 (pb : alk. paper) | ISBN 9781512450347 (eb pdf)
Subjects: LCSH: Refuse collection—Juvenile literature.
Classification: LCC TD794 .K46 2018 (print) | LCC TD794 (ebook) | DDC 628.4/42—dc23

LC record available at https://lccn.loc.gov/2016044369

Manufactured in the United States of America
1 – CG – 7/15/17

LERNER
SOURCE™

Expand learning beyond the printed book. Download free, complementary educational resources for this book from our website, www.lernerresource.com.

Table of
Contents

Garbage Collectors

Garbage collectors work hard.

They pick up trash and recycling.

Why are there different bins?

These workers drive

garbage trucks.

Some trucks have an arm.

The arm lifts the bins.

Some trucks do not have an arm.

Then a worker dumps the bins.

He does this all day.

Garbage collectors work

on the streets.

They wear bright shirts.

The shirts help drivers

see them.

They wear gloves too.

Gloves keep their hands clean.

How might gloves keep a worker's hands safe?

Garbage collectors also

work in other places.

They pick up trash in parks.

They pick up trash

for businesses.

The truck is full.

Collectors go to a station.

Recycling is sorted here.

What might they sort?

Garbage collectors have

tough jobs.

They work hard to keep

places clean.

Garbage Collector Tools

bright shirt

gloves

truck

22

Picture Glossary

bins

containers that
hold trash

recycling

trash that
is reused

sorted

similar things
grouped together

trash

items that have
been thrown away

23

Read More

Bullard, Lisa. *Rally for Recycling*. Minneapolis: Millbrook Press, 2012.

Meister, Cari. *Garbage Trucks*. Minneapolis: Jump, 2014.

Owings, Lisa. *From Garbage to Compost*. Minneapolis: Lerner Publications, 2017.

Index

Photo Credits